LESS IS MORE

LESS IS MORE

LESS OF ME, MORE OF GOD!

David Hancox

Copyright © 2023 David Hancox

All rights reserved.

ISBN: 9798870335216
Imprint: Independently published

All Scripture quotations, unless otherwise indicated, are taken from the Holy Bible, New International Version®, NIV®. Copyright ©1973, 1978, 1984, 2011 by Biblica, Inc.™ Used by permission of Zondervan. All rights reserved worldwide. www.zondervan.comThe "NIV" and "New International Version" are trademarks registered in the United States Patent and Trademark Office by Biblica, Inc.™

Cover Image © David Hancox

Contents

Introduction	8
1. It makes a difference.	11
2. Seven men! What do they tell us about God.	21
3. Less looks like?	27
4. Will people say that you were a pointer?	35
5. Prepare the way.	43
6. Second guessing.	51
7. Devotional.	59
8. Seven days of prayer.	62
9. Closing thoughts.	69
10. Notes.	71

LESS IS MORE

LESS OF ME, MORE OF GOD!

"Choosing 'less of me, more of God' unlocks a transformative spiritual path, fostering humility and openness to divine guidance, enriching lives with boundless wisdom and purpose."

Dedication

In humble gratitude to the Divine for the gift of wisdom and guidance throughout the creation of "Less is More," I offer my sincerest thanks. Your presence has illuminated every word, shaping this work into a reflection of your boundless insight.

To my beloved family, especially my cherished wife Tina, and our six remarkable children - James, Bradley, Thomas, Noah, Daisy, and Poppy - your unwavering support and love have been the cornerstone of my inspiration. Your patience during the countless hours spent writing is a testament to your understanding and belief in this endeavour.

To the congregation at Hope Church Oldbury, your encouragement has been a beacon of strength. Your faith and support have infused this work with a sense of purpose and determination, guiding me through moments of doubt.

May this offering, shaped by gratitude and love, resonate with those who encounter its pages, echoing the spirit of simplicity and depth.

I pray the lord will continue to bless you all,

Dave.

Introduction

In the whispers of ancient texts, there echoes a profound truth—less is more with God. In delving into the life of John the Baptist, we unearth a narrative steeped in this guiding principle. But beyond the confines of history, this principle resonates as a beacon guiding our own life's journey.

John the Baptist, a figure often veiled in the shadows of larger narratives, embodies an ethos worth emulating. Consider the legacy he left—perhaps not one of grandeur or earthly accolades, but one of profound significance. What echoes in the records of time about John is not his personal acclaim, but his singular focus: pointing humanity towards the Divine. "Prepare the way of the Lord." A simple directive that, on the surface, seems to beckon us to don the attire of road builders. Yet, beneath this literal interpretation lies a call far more profound. John wasn't a constructor of physical paths but a precursor to a spiritual awakening. His message wasn't about bricks and mortar but about hearts and spirits, paving the way for the arrival of something far greater than himself.

In the flux of time, we encounter John at a pivotal juncture, imprisoned and grappling with uncertainty. Even he, who stood as a beacon of faith, found himself second-guessing.

In the dimness of captivity, doubts clouded his mind, questioning the very essence of the Messiah he had devotedly heralded.

As we unravel the enigma of John's existence, we unearth not a life of opulence but a life of purpose. His narrative invites us to ponder our own legacy—are we leaving behind a trail that points others toward greater truths? Are we, amidst our doubts and uncertainties, still resolute in our devotion to guiding others toward the Divine?

In these pages, we embark on a journey—exploring the life of John the Baptist not merely as a historical figure but as a timeless exemplar of the "less is more" ethos. Let us traverse the terrains of his existence, drawing wisdom and inspiration for our own pilgrimage towards a deeper connection with the Divine. For in the echoes of John's legacy, we find a whispered truth—less, indeed, is more when it comes to leading others toward the profound and eternal.

It makes a difference

We're all familiar with the saying "less is more." In my recent Bible readings centred around John the Baptist, a particular verse struck me in Matthew 11:11, where Jesus himself proclaims John as the greatest among those born of women.
Pause and consider the weight of that statement.

Amidst the roster of faith heroes—Abel, Enoch, Abraham, Noah, Moses, David, and the revered prophets like Isaiah, Daniel, and others—Jesus specifically highlights John's unparalleled greatness. It's a thought that lingers, urging deeper contemplation.
This led me to delve into John the Baptist's life. What resonated profoundly was the recurring theme of 'less being greater than more' in God's eyes, a motif embedded in his life.

The world consistently bombards us with the belief that 'more' equates to greatness—more possessions, more debts, more acquisitions, more wealth. It's the narrative of the world's economy where big businesses chase billions, aiming for even more the following year.

Yet, John's life underscores a different example—a perspective that stands in contrast to the world's clamour for more.

In John's story, I found a consistent echo of a profound truth: Less holds more significance in God's economy. This is a recurrent theme throughout Scripture, but John the Baptist exemplifies it vividly.

The world's logic insists on the necessity for more—more possessions, more debts, more acquisitions, and more wealth. Yet, John's life attests to the contrary. It's a radical deviation from the world's narrative, emphasising that less, when aligned with God's principles, holds greater weight than the world's 'more.'
This division in perspectives—more versus less—encapsulates a fundamental distinction between the world's values and God's design, a theme rooted deeply in John the Baptist's life.

However, God's economy doesn't conform to these worldly standards. In God's economy and theology, the principle of 'less is greater than more' holds true. Recall the words of Jesus: "the last shall be first and the first last." This echoes the idea that less holds more significance in God's perspective.

Jesus consistently emphasises the power within weakness and the strength derived from it. This underscores the concept that 'less is more.' He also teaches about the elevation of the humble and the humbling of the elevated. It's a recurring theme in Jesus's teachings that less often holds more weight in God's eyes. This principle of 'less is greater than more with God' was a driving force in John the Baptist's life. It's a theme worth exploring, so let us delve into it further.

Let's take a look at our initial passage from Luke 1:12-17 to shed light on this concept.

12 When Zechariah saw him, he was startled and was gripped with fear.

13 But the angel said to him: "Do not be afraid, Zechariah; your prayer has been heard. Your wife Elizabeth will bear you a son, and you are to give him the name John.

14 He will be a joy and delight to you, and many will rejoice because of his birth,

15 for he will be great in the sight of the Lord. He is never to take wine or other fermented drink, and he will be filled with the Holy Spirit even from birth.

16 Many of the people of Israel will he bring back to the Lord their God.

17 And he will go on before the Lord, in the spirit and power of Elijah, to turn the hearts of the fathers to their children and the disobedient to the wisdom of the righteous--to make ready a people prepared for the Lord."

God executes His plan according to His timing and method. It's crucial for us to align with His guidance rather than resist it.

As I yield, the result is that God gains more control over my life while I willingly relinquish control. This underscores the principle that 'less yields more' in God's realm.

John the Baptist's life was encompassed by a remarkable plan crafted by God. Prophet Isaiah, seven hundred years before John's birth, foretold this divine design for John's life.

Isaiah 40:3

A voice of one calling: "In the desert prepare the way for the LORD; make straight in the wilderness a highway for our God.

This plan was affirmed in the Book of Matthew as the divine blueprint for John the Baptist's life.

Matthew 3:1-3

1 In those days John the Baptist came, preaching in the Desert of Judea

2 and saying, "Repent, for the kingdom of heaven is near."

3 This is he who was spoken of through the prophet Isaiah: "A voice of one calling in the desert, 'Prepare the way for the Lord, make straight paths for him.'"

You might argue that John the Baptist was exceptional because no one born of a woman is greater, as just mentioned. But consider the rest of that verse—it continues, "*yet he who is least in the kingdom of heaven is greater than he.*" Jesus implies that despite John's greatness, he isn't uniquely special in the context of the Kingdom of Heaven.

John the Baptist shared common ground with us—all of us possess the potential for the same greatness that John exhibited. What made John remarkable was his decision to embrace and follow God's plan for his life. He wasn't obligated, yet he willingly chose to align with God's purpose.

This leads us to a crucial realisation: God holds a plan for each of our lives.

For I know the plans I have for you," declares the LORD, "plans to prosper you and not to harm you, plans to give you hope and a future.

As Jeremiah 29:11 affirms, there's a divine blueprint for you and me just as there was for John the Baptist. Similar to John the Baptist, God has a distinct plan for both your life and mine. We face the decision of whether to align with this divine plan or not. When I choose to walk in accordance with God's plan, I willingly yield more control of my life to God. Conversely, if I reject His plan, I seize more control while diminishing God's influence in my life.

John the Baptist opted to surrender control to God, and similarly, we should consider giving God authority in our lives because in God's economy, less yields more. The blessings of life often emerge when God holds the reins, and we relinquish control.

Every prayer serves as a testament to the principle that less holds greater significance in God's realm. I pray because I acknowledge my incapacity to alter my circumstances, whereas God possesses the ability to intervene. Consider this: when we believe we can tackle a situation ourselves, do we pray? Usually not; we handle it independently. Prayer comes into play when I recognise my limitations in handling a situation.

Therefore, prayer serves as a reminder that 'less is more.' It signifies that I turn to prayer because I lack the solution, but God holds it. It's an acknowledgment of my lesser position, acknowledging God's greater ability to handle the situation. In God's domain, less often holds more weight.

In the first chapter of Luke, we encounter the story of two righteous Jewish individuals, Elizabeth and Zechariah.

Luke 1:6-7

6 Both of them were upright in the sight of God, observing all the Lord's commandments and regulations blamelessly.

7 But they had no children, because Elizabeth was barren; and they were both well along in years.

They were described as faithfully observing the Lord's commandments without fault. One might assume that everything would be flawless in their lives given their dedication to God, but that wasn't the case. Simply living for God doesn't guarantee a perfect life.

Elizabeth and Zechariah faced a significant challenge—they couldn't conceive for two reasons. Firstly, Elizabeth was unable to conceive, and secondly, both were elderly, well beyond the years of childbearing.

Their situation presented an insurmountable hurdle. There was nothing they could do to change it.

Could they seek medical assistance for this issue? No. Could Elizabeth improve her diet or Zechariah exercise in hopes of resolving it? No. They found themselves in a situation where human effort was limited, but the scope of what God could accomplish was vast.

So, what did they do? In Verse 13, we're informed that their prayer had been heard.

This highlights the importance of vocalising one's prayers to have them acknowledged. True prayer revolves around diminishing one's self-importance and amplifying reliance on God. It's another illustration that in God's realm, 'less' often means 'more.'

The route to genuine greatness with the Lord, entails reducing the influence of the world within you.

for he will be great in the sight of the Lord. He is never to take wine or other fermented drink, and he will be filled with the Holy Spirit even from birth. Luke 1:15

The angel Gabriel didn't instruct Zechariah to cultivate specific traits or immerse John in ancient teachings. Instead, Gabriel urged Zechariah to shield John from worldly influences. It's about having less of the world and making room for more of God.

This aligns with the message in Romans—do not conform to the patterns of this world. The essence here is clear: it's impossible to achieve greatness in God's sight while harbouring excessive worldly influences in your life.

Do not love the world or anything in the world. If anyone loves the world, the love of the Father is not in him. 1 John 2:15

It's easy to understand why the church lacks the greatness and power it once held? It's because it has become too entangled with worldly elements. Some churches resemble entertainment venues, blurring the line between spiritual worship and secular entertainment.

I've heard of worship leaders who prioritise putting on a spectacle rather than truly seeking the Spirit's guidance.

Moreover, the absence of Christians greatly esteemed in God's eyes often roots in their entanglement with worldly influences.

When was the last time you earnestly prayed to remove certain things from your life, rather than asking for more?

Our prayers frequently ask for additional blessings rather than requesting to shed worldly attachments.

When you diminish yourself and allow more of God to manifest, your influence on the kingdom of God becomes powerful and far-reaching.

Luke 1:16-17

16 Many of the people of Israel will he bring back to the Lord their God.

17 And he will go on before the Lord, in the spirit and power of Elijah, to turn the hearts of the fathers to their children and the disobedient to the wisdom of the righteous--to make ready a people prepared for the Lord."

It's concerning if people choose not to embrace Christianity because, despite knowing you're a believer, they see minimal distinction between you and themselves.

John the Baptist stood out precisely because there was less of his own presence and more of God's presence in his life. This authenticity drew people to the wilderness to hear his message, and through this, he successfully guided them back to God.

Adopting the idea of 'less of us, more of God' serves as a potent cue. When we diminish our ego, self-focus, and material cravings, we open room for the divine to thrive in our lives.

This space of humility and surrender offers an avenue for a profound spiritual connection, inner tranquility, and the ability to be guided by God's grace along our journey.
Let's wholeheartedly welcome the principle of 'less is more' in our relationship with God.

Seven men! What do they tell us about God.

Throughout Scripture, a recurring theme unfolds, revealing that 'less is more with God.' Let's examine the words of Jesus Himself to grasp this concept. In Matthew 10:39, Jesus emphasises that losing one's life for His sake leads to finding it—a prime example of 'less (losing your life) is more (finding it).'
Likewise, in John 12:24, Jesus likens a single grain's sacrifice to produce an abundance, emphasising the principle that 'less (one grain) is more (much grain).'

Another poignant reflection occurs when Jesus questions what it profits a person to amass worldly possessions yet lose their soul—a clear demonstration that 'less is more.'

As I delve into the life of John the Baptist, I've noticed this theme profoundly echoing his existence. We glimpsed it previously when discussing the announcement of his birth by the angel Gabriel. As we explore John's ministry, this theme resurfaces prominently. Intriguingly, the passage introducing John's ministry presents seven individuals, arousing my curiosity about their significance.

In this chapter, our focus will be on exploring Luke 3:1-4.

Luke 3:1-4

1 In the fifteenth year of the reign of Tiberius Caesar--when Pontius Pilate was governor of Judea, Herod tetrarch of Galilee, his brother Philip tetrarch of Iturea and Traconitis, and Lysanias tetrarch of Abilene--

2 during the high priesthood of Annas and Caiaphas, the word of God came to John son of Zechariah in the desert.

3 He went into all the country around the Jordan, preaching a baptism of repentance for the forgiveness of sins.

4 As is written in the book of the words of Isaiah the prophet: "A voice of one calling in the desert, 'Prepare the way for the Lord, make straight paths for him.

Verses 1-2 introduce seven notable individuals, each widely recognised across Israel. Despite the potential impact if any of them were to surrender their life to Christ and become Jesus' forerunner, the Word of God reaches John in the desert, making him the chosen forerunner. It's a powerful testament to the principle that 'less is more' in God's divine plan.

Consider this scenario: Out of seven widely known individuals, God chose John, a man dwelling in the desert, to deliver the most momentous announcement in human history!

sending Jesus to address our sin predicament. What does this signify? It reveals that God's methods diverge from ours. We often attempt to confine God's actions by presuming He can only operate in specific ways. However, God's capacity to act in our lives is boundless. Regardless of the challenges we face, we must bear in mind that God operates in limitless ways.

Isaiah 55:8

8 "For my thoughts are not your thoughts, neither are your ways my ways," declares the LORD.

Verses 1-2 introduce seven men, with five wielding substantial control over governance, while Annas and Caiaphas hold dominion within the Jewish religious structure. From a human standpoint, it appears unsuitable for the Messiah to emerge at this time. Humanly speaking, the situation is restrictive.

    The government staunchly opposes anyone claiming to be the Messiah, reserving the singular place for Caesar as king. Additionally, the religious system operates as a profitable machine for its leaders, leaving no space for a Messiah to revolutionise the established order. This juncture appears bleak and seemingly impossible in human terms.

One might argue that Jesus should have arrived before Roman authority firmly gripped Israel or before religious leaders entrenched themselves in power and greed.
However, as Romans 5:6 states, the timing might seem improbable from our perspective, but it is significant in God's plan.

You see, at just the right time, when we were still powerless, Christ died for the ungodly.
Romans 5:6

If Jesus' death occurred at the precise moment, then his birth also aligned with that timing, despite being amidst the darkest period.

However, therein lies the hopeful news for us: God steps into our most dire moments, amidst darkness and when hope seems scarce. Our instinct is for God to arrive at the onset of a problem, not when we're almost losing all hope. Yet, often, it's precisely in those desperate moments that God chooses to reveal Himself.

This illustrates the difference between God's timing and our own. But this realisation brings good news—it encourages us never to abandon hope, recognising that God's timing surpasses our comprehension and brings light in the darkest hours.

Verses 1-2 introduce seven men, all located in populated regions.

However, John the Baptist stands out, situated in the wilderness around the Jordan—an unexpected place for Jesus' forerunner. Typically, one might anticipate finding such a figure in populous areas rather than in the desert. Yet, the remarkable news is that **we can encounter God anywhere.**

It's a testament to the principle that 'less is more' with God, revealing His presence and influence even in the most unlikely places.

3 He went into all the country around the Jordan, preaching a baptism of repentance for the forgiveness of sins.

4 As is written in the book of the words of Isaiah the prophet: "A voice of one calling in the desert, 'Prepare the way for the Lord, make straight paths for him. Luke 3:3-4

I encountered Jesus while working at a territorial army base in 1991. My wife Tina discovered Jesus at a Billy Graham crusade held at Villa Park. The Apostle Paul encountered God along the Damascus Road. Similarly, the Ethiopian eunuch found Jesus in the desert. Today's Good News is that encountering Jesus doesn't confine itself to the church house. From what I've seen, He meets you wherever you are.

The introduction of these seven men by the Holy Spirit serves as a profound reminder that God's ways diverge from ours.

His timing transcends ours, and His presence isn't limited to any specific setting. This display underscores that Jesus isn't restricted to populous places or the confines of a church house; rather, He can manifest Himself anywhere and meet us exactly where we are.

So my question to you is: what are you going to do about it?

Less looks like?

In the past two chapters, my goal was to emphasise a crucial Biblical principle that we must weave into our lives. This principle is fundamental: 'Less is more with God.' While it guided John the Baptist's life, it should similarly shape our own. Jesus vividly illustrates this principle in Matthew 19:29.

"And everyone who has left houses or brothers or sisters or father or mother or wife or children or fields for my sake will receive a hundred times as much and will inherit eternal life."

"Less is more with God."

For me to grasp the concept of having less in my life so that God can have more,
I need specific, tangible illustrations to better understand the idea.

In our Scripture for this chapter, John the Baptist provides three concrete examples of what less looks like."

Luke 3:2-8

2 ... the word of God came to John son of Zechariah in the desert.

3 He went into all the country around the Jordan, preaching a baptism of repentance for the forgiveness of sins.

4 As is written in the book of the words of Isaiah the prophet: "A voice of one calling in the desert, 'Prepare the way for the Lord, make straight paths for him.

5 Every valley shall be filled in, every mountain and hill made low. The crooked roads shall become straight, the rough ways smooth.

6 And all mankind will see God's salvation.'"

7 John said to the crowds coming out to be baptised by him, "You brood of vipers! Who warned you to flee from the coming wrath?

8 Produce fruit in keeping with repentance. And do not begin to say to yourselves, 'We have Abraham as our father.' For I tell you that out of these stones God can raise up children for Abraham.

Less entails following God's instructions on where to go, what to do, and what to say.
... the word of God came to John, the son of Zechariah, while he was in the desert.

In the Scripture, we witness John's life before the word of God reached him: residing in the desert, clothed in camel-hair attire, and subsisting on locusts and wild honey.

He appears as a solitary figure. If he lived in our times, we might describe him as living off the grid—perhaps even eligible for his own TV show or YouTube channel! I'm certain that someone like Ben Fogle would pay John a visit to film an episode of "New Lives in the Wild."Witness the profound transformation that unfolded when God commanded John to go!

Once a solitary figure in the wild, heeding the call meant leaving behind the familiar and venturing into the vast expanse surrounding the Jordan.

Living alone in the desert, who would you converse with all day long? Nobody. Consider it—living in isolation, there's no one to engage with day in and day out, correct? Not a soul. Yet, John seized the opportunity to deliver sermons. Responding to God's call for one-on-one conversations is one matter, but addressing a crowd is an entirely different challenge, particularly for someone accustomed to solitary life in the desert, where interactions are absent.

If you doubt this, I invite you to step up to the podium of your church and experience it firsthand. John departed from his comfort zone in the wilderness and obediently fulfilled God's command. He preached a message advocating baptism for the forgiveness of sins. This message posed a significant challenge, as it diverged from traditional Jewish practices—where circumcision, not baptism, held prominence.

In Jewish tradition, baptism was associated with non-Jews, Gentiles who converted to Judaism. For a self-respecting Jew, adopting baptism equated to aligning with the outsiders converting to Judaism. However, despite this discomfort, God instructed John to preach this message to the Jews, thrusting him into an uncomfortable position. He had to step out of his comfort zone to deliver this unconventional message.

Do you know why the church lacks a substantial influence in the world? It has remained within its comfort zone.
If you, as a Christian, find satisfaction in preserving your present spiritual state without actively pursuing growth, you've securely nestled into your comfort zone.
Be ready, as it shouldn't surprise you if God encourages you to step beyond the confines of that comfort zone.

Living with less means living a life that isn't solely centred around oneself. Our world often preaches a self-absorbed philosophy, constantly bombarding us with messages that revolve around "me."

If you doubt this, simply switch on the TV and notice the plethora of commercials implying that you deserve what they're selling. Or visit any bookstore and observe the multitude of books in the self-help section. You might come across books like those from one of my favourite authors, Joel Osteen. (NOT!)

In his book, "The Power of I Am," the author emphasises...
"Stop focusing on your weaknesses and instead proclaim the power of 'I am.' Say I am strong, I am healthy, I am blessed, I am beautiful, I am prosperous." Which is all well and good, but who's the emphasis on? Me.
But consider the teachings of the Apostle Paul...

But he said to me, "My grace is sufficient for you, for my power is made perfect in weakness." Therefore I will boast all the more gladly of my weaknesses, so that

the power of Christ may rest upon me.

2 Corinthians 12:9

The world preaches a message of "me, me, me," but in our passage of scripture Luke 3:4 which is quoted from Isaiah, a different narrative emerges—one echoed throughout the Bible: life isn't solely about us.
John the Baptist is described as a "voice of one calling in the desert." There's no mention of his name, his relation to Jesus, or his parents. No accolades are given to John the Baptist because the focus isn't on him.

Admittedly, there are churches and individuals within Christianity who emphasise themselves more than God. When a church or a Christian fixates on their own actions, it leaves little space for God's work to unfold. This mindset often stems from pride, and as James 4:6 reveals, the Scriptures speak about God's stance on pride.

"God opposes the proud but gives grace to the humble."

Being less means attributing no credit to myself and giving all the credit to God. Charles Spurgeon, the renowned preacher, once stated, "When a person is genuinely humble, never seeking even a speck of praise, there's almost no limit to what God will do for them." This concept illustrates that less is indeed more when it comes to God.

Allow me to be unequivocal here, friends. Unlike some pastors and preachers who believe the Bible is centred on themselves, I'm sorry to say it's not. It has always been and will always be about Him—Jesus, the one and only, the Great "I Am."

Being "less" resembles a person who cares enough about others to speak the truth, even if it places them in an uncomfortable position. Let's recall the message conveyed in Luke 3:7-8.

7 John said to the crowds coming out to be baptised by him, "You brood of vipers! Who warned you to flee from the coming wrath?

8 Produce fruit in keeping with repentance. And do not begin to say to yourselves, 'We have Abraham as our father.' For I tell you that out of these stones God can raise up children for Abraham.

Imagine John the Baptist, a solitary figure in the desert. In that desolate landscape, he likely encountered few individuals and engaged in minimal conversation on a regular day. Then, the Spirit of God summons him. He journeys across the region near the Jordan, encountering people he deliberately avoided while in the desert. Now, not only is he conversing with them, but he's also preaching, engaging in dialogues he never had during his time in the desert.

We now see that John is not just encountering people; he's actively engaging in conversations and delivering truths, even if they might provoke anger. Labelling them a "brood of vipers" likely stirs frustration and resentment. He further challenges their belief in their special status as descendants of Abraham, emphasising that God can create descendants from stones.

This makes one wonder how many individuals have sidestepped difficult conversations about Christ with family and friends simply to avoid uncomfortable situations.

Today, I am asking you to move out of your comfort zone.

Today, I am challenging your church to move out of its comfort zone.

Less can only happen when, we move out of our comfort zones.

John the Baptist was able to do that. Can you?

Will people say that you were a pointer?

The Book of James compares life to a fleeting vapour, a truth that becomes more evident as I age. I recall going to bed young and waking up feeling old; time seems to slip away. They say you're old when you check the obituaries first in the newspaper, and I admit, I've glanced at those myself in the free newspapers that come through the door, curious if I recognise any names.

Reading what people share about their loved ones in those pages is oddly captivating. So, naturally, I ponder: "What will be said about me when I'm no longer here?" Those who know me might describe me in different ways. My wife Tina might say I was a devoted husband, while others might see me as someone who worked a lot. Some in my congregation might say I was a good pastor or a faithful Christian. Our drummer Skip might call me crazy, and Elder Steve caveman clarke might remember the times, I gave him a hard time from the pulpit. Honestly, I can't predict what people will say when I'm gone, but here's to hoping we'll all be raptured together. Amen.

John the Baptist set an example I admire, and I hope to embody his spirit. He was known for directing people toward Christ. My wish is that the same could be said of each of us: that we were pointers to Christ. You've heard the phrase "it's rude to point," and in many cases, that holds true. But in the context I'll be discussing in this chapter, it's essential to point. A pointer, in this sense, is someone more concerned about the person they're directing others to than about themselves. Once again, it underscores the principle that less is more with God, a driving force in John the Baptist's life.

In the Scripture we're exploring, it's evident that John the Baptist was a pointer. Upon seeing Jesus approaching, he declares to those around him, "Look, the Lamb of God, who takes away the sin of the world!" I envision him gesturing, pointing directly towards Christ as he speaks. John the Baptist was indeed a pointer, and likewise, we should aspire to be pointers. I'll delve into three compelling reasons from our text to support this.

John 1:29-34

29 The next day John saw Jesus coming toward him and said, "Look, the Lamb of God, who takes away the sin of the world!

30 This is the one I meant when I said, 'A man who comes after me has surpassed me because he was before me.'

31 I myself did not know him, but the reason I came baptising with water was that he might be revealed to Israel."

32 Then John gave this testimony: "I saw the Spirit come down from heaven as a dove and remain on him.

33 I would not have known him, except that the one who sent me to baptise with water told me, 'The man on whom you see the Spirit come down and remain is he who will baptise with the Holy Spirit.'

34 I have seen and I testify that this is the Son of God."

We need to be pointers because the way to redemption is narrow, and unless we show others, they may miss it. Open your Bible to John 1:29 and highlight the phrase "the Lamb of God." It's essential to note that John the Baptist didn't say "a lamb of God" or "here comes one of the Lambs of God," suggesting there might be more than one. He specifically stated "the Lamb of God," emphasising the singularity of this reference.

When there's only one Lamb of God, it signifies there's only one path to salvation. That's precisely what Jesus teaches us in...John 14:6

Jesus answered, "I am the way and the truth and the life. No one comes to the Father except through me.

The Bible describes redemption as a narrow path that many will overlook, opting instead for the broad gate leading to destruction. But why is that? Society discourages pointing, but the Bible insists that we must. Without Christians guiding the way, many might miss the path to eternal life, choosing alternative routes in their pursuit of salvation.

People often believe there are various paths to salvation, like when Pope Francis mentioned on October 5th 2021 that "Religions Are All 'Different Ways of Coming to God'." My friend VJ once followed another path in the Hindu faith until he encountered the Lamb of God. Now, he fervently shares that the only way to the Father in heaven is through surrendering to Jesus, the king of kings and lord of lords.

Pay attention: Without Christians pointing the way, many may overlook the path to eternal life!

We must be pointers! because this world spreads a lot of misinformation about Jesus. In John 1:30, John the Baptist acknowledges that Jesus was born after him, with an age difference of about six months. However, John makes an intriguing statement: Jesus has surpassed me because he was before me. It seems paradoxical, considering their birth sequence. But the Bible holds the key to unraveling this mystery.

John 1:1-3

1 In the beginning was the Word, and the Word was with God, and the Word was God.

2 He was with God in the beginning.

3 Through him all things were made; without him nothing was made that has been made.

John 8:56-58

56 Your father Abraham rejoiced at the thought of seeing my day; he saw it and was glad."

57 "You are not yet fifty years old," the Jews said to him, "and you have seen Abraham!"

58 "I tell you the truth," Jesus answered, "before Abraham was born, I am!"

The Bible is crystal clear on this point: Jesus has always existed. However, in this world, some religious groups claim that Jesus is a created being, introducing confusion to those without the guidance of the Holy Spirit.

Is Jesus eternal or a created entity? Our responsibility is to direct others towards the Jesus presented in the Bible, not the version crafted by specific religious doctrines. The Jesus of the Bible is eternal, and that's the focal point we ought to highlight. If we neglect to do so, some might miss comprehending the profound significance of Jesus and the salvation He offers, leading to the loss of the hope we cherish—that one day, a transformation awaits us all in an instant.

If we fail to point people to Christ, they will miss the remarkable promise found in Revelation 21:3-7.

3 "And I heard a loud voice from the throne saying, "Look! God's dwelling place is now among the people, and he will dwell with them. They will be his people, and God himself will be with them and be their God.

4 'He will wipe every tear from their eyes. There will be no more death' or mourning or crying or pain, for the old order of things has passed away."

5 He who was seated on the throne said, "I am making everything new!" Then he said, "Write this down, for these words are trustworthy and true."

6 He said to me: "It is done. I am the Alpha and the Omega, the Beginning and the End. To the thirsty I will give water without cost from the spring of the water of life.

7 Those who are victorious will inherit all this, and I will be their God and they will be my children."

We must serve as guides because the Bible reveals Jesus as the Redeemer, the source of eternal life. But if people aren't familiar with the Bible, how will they recognise Jesus as the one who offers them eternal life?

In the Old Testament, the Spirit would empower someone for a specific task and then depart. However, in our passage, John 1:32-34, John the Baptist describes the Holy Spirit descending on Jesus and remaining with Him permanently. It's noted that this person will baptise with the Holy Spirit, information that John attributes to God the Father. So, the crucial question arises: Did John the Baptist fabricate this revelation?

Well the answer to that question is no.
Let us read Isaiah 11:1-2

1 "A shoot will come up from the stump of Jesse; from his roots a Branch will bear fruit.

2 The Spirit of the LORD will rest on him-- the Spirit of wisdom and of understanding, the Spirit of counsel and of power, the Spirit of knowledge and of the fear of the LORD--"

John the Baptist's testimony aligns with the Old Testament's prophecy about Jesus as the Son of God. It reinforces the reliability and truthfulness of the Bible, which is what we should be directing people towards.

    The reality is, we all serve as pointers guiding others towards Christ. You might encounter questions like, "Why should I follow your religion or your Jesus when there's truth in other religions?" It's true, there may be elements of truth in various beliefs, but what sets Jesus apart is His declaration: "I am the way, the truth, and the life. No one comes to the Father except through me."

    So, who will you point towards Christ? Consider creating a list of unsaved loved ones. Dedicate time to pray for them every day, asking God to grant you opportunities and the right words to point them towards Jesus. Each person you lead towards Christ makes an eternal difference.

Prepare the way.

In Matthew 3:3, the prophetic words of Isaiah state that John the Baptist will call the people to "prepare the way of the Lord" and "make His paths straight." But what exactly does that entail? Is John suggesting that the people engage in road construction or seek employment with the local council to fix potholes? I carefully examined John's teachings to understand precisely what he meant by "prepare the way." It's indeed about roadwork, but not the physical kind; it's about tending to our hearts. His message centred on repentance —a call to cleanse our hearts in anticipation of his arrival. Essentially, it's heart roadwork.

Consider the lyrics of the Christmas hymn "Joy to the World":

"Joy to the world, the Lord has come
Let earth receive her King
Let every heart prepare Him room (Do the Road work)
And heaven and nature sing, and heaven and nature sing
And heaven, and heaven and nature sing."

This understanding of "preparing the way of the Lord" raises another important question: How do I do that?

let's delve into the process of spiritual roadwork for our hearts. To kick-start this exploration, let's turn our attention to the Gospel of John, specifically chapter 3, verses 25-30.

25 An argument developed between of John's disciples and a certain Jew over the matter of ceremonial washing.

26 They came to John and said to him, "Rabbi, that man who was with you on the other side of the Jordan--the one you testified about--well, he is baptising, and everyone is going to him."

27 To this John replied, "A man can receive only what is given him from heaven.

28 You yourselves can testify that I said, 'I am not the Christ but am sent ahead of him.'

29 The bride belongs to the bridegroom. The friend who attends the bridegroom waits and listens for him, and is full of joy when he hears the bridegroom's voice. That joy is mine, and it is now complete.

30 He must become greater; I must become less. (Less is more)

In readying my heart, purity of intention is vital. My motivation must be solely focused on preparing my heart for Christ; any personal agenda would distract from this essential endeavour.Let's examine the differences in motivations between John the Baptist and his followers. In verses 22 and 23 of this chapter, it's revealed that Jesus and his disciples were performing baptisms in the Judean countryside, while John and his followers were doing the same in the region of Salim. This points to a time when Jesus and John had similar ministries running simultaneously.

This highlights the difference in motivation between John's disciples and John the Baptist himself. The disciples approached John, referencing the one he testified about without mentioning his name—Jesus, the Son of God as acknowledged by John.

Moreover, they express concern that Jesus is doing precisely what they've been doing—baptising. It feels like He's imitating our concept. Why doesn't He embark on something unique? Furthermore, everyone is flocking to Him, and it seems He's becoming more prominent than us.

In this religious context, the disciples' motivation appears to stem not from seeking God but from jealousy. They seem inclined to elevate their group as the most prominent and superior. If this situation unfolded in the present day, their conversation might resemble something like this:

"What if we set up a trendy coffee spot by the river? We could arrange some bistro chairs, add a fog machine for an atmospheric touch."

The motivation of John the Baptist's disciples is entirely misplaced. Consider John the Baptist's motivation here. He explicitly states, "I am only a man sent ahead of Christ." He acknowledges God's supremacy, recognising that he isn't divine. His motivation is pure, focused on seeking God. This narrative serves as a reminder that individuals attending church today do so with diverse motivations.

Some attend with pure intentions, genuinely seeking God. Others may come to impress a partner or avoid negative judgments. Some arrive hoping to strike a deal with God, seeking solutions to their problems. A few attend seeking business opportunities, while others come simply to cause trouble. To ready our hearts for God, we must assess our reasons for going to church. Ultimately, a pure motive is the only one that aligns with God's will.

I am here because I want to know Him!

I am here because I need a saviour!

I am here because I want to grow in my relationship with Him!

And remember, God can see your motivation.

Proper motivation I decrease, and Christ increases. Less is more!

Improper motivation I increase, and Christ decreases in my life.

To prepare my heart, I must comprehend my rightful place in Christ and steadfastly remain in that position. Remember when you were a child in your home? Whenever adults visited, your parents likely instructed you not to interrupt their conversations. You had the choice to sit quietly among the adults or go play in your room. The message was clear: understand your place and stick to it.

In many families today, there's chaos. And why? It's because family members have forgotten their rightful positions at home. Often, it's the children who seem to be in charge, and the parents end up following their lead. This isn't the way it should be, and the consequence is disorder within the household.

John's disciples lost sight of their place; they wanted their group to take the lead, to be in control. But John remained grounded in his rightful position. He tells them, 'I'm not the Christ, but I'm honoured to be sent by Him. I understand where I stand!'
When you mention that everyone is going to Christ instead of us, it's because He's the groom of the church.

All I am is the best man, so I'm here to witness and celebrate the beautiful relationship between the bride and the groom.
Today's churches face turmoil because people have forgotten their rightful place.
They believe it's their church and theirs to control. It's not 'my church' or 'your church'—it's Jesus' Church! Once we forget that, chaos creeps in.

Now, consider our personal lives. When we start dictating to God what we want, we're stepping out of our rightful place.
Consider your prayers—are they mostly about what you want from God, or are they about what you can do for Him today? Finding our proper position involves aligning our hearts in service rather than self-centred requests.
That's key to preparing our hearts.

To ready my heart, I must firmly understand that there's no room for negotiation regarding what it takes to maintain a genuine relationship with God. Let us look at John 3:30

He <u>must</u> become greater; I <u>must</u> become less.

Turn to John 3:30 in your Bible and underline two crucial words in that verse: 'must' and 'must.' It doesn't suggest that He should increase and I should decrease. Nor does it propose that it would be beneficial if He increased while I decreased.

Instead, it states unequivocally that He must increase and I must decrease. When it's a matter of must, where is the room for negotiation? There isn't any.

When it comes to salvation, there's no room for negotiation. There's only one pathway to salvation, and that is through the Lord Jesus Christ. He unequivocally states, 'I am the way, the truth, and the Life; no one comes to the Father except through Me.

There's no space for manoeuvring in how you live your life. Romans 12:1 makes it clear:

'Therefore, I urge you, brothers, in view of God's mercy, to offer your bodies as living sacrifices, holy and pleasing to God—this is your spiritual act of worship.'

Chaos creeps in when we seek leeway in salvation, thinking there might be another way. But the truth is clear: He must increase, and I must decrease. There's no room for negotiation. Less is more.

Chaos doesn't just stem from salvation; it emerges when we attempt to find loopholes in our daily Christian lives.

Ever thought, 'On which days do I need to be a living sacrifice this week?' Truth is, every day. Remove yourself from that altar, attempt to run your life for even a day, and witness the chaos that follows.

If your life feels chaotic today, it could be due to three things that create potholes in your heart:

wrong motivation, misunderstanding your proper position, and seeking wiggle room where none exists.

What's the solution? Jesus, and Jesus alone! Consider His invitation in Matthew 11:28

'Come to me, all you who are weary and burdened, and I will give you rest.'

Second Guessing.

We have arrived at the concluding chapter of 'Less is More,' and my desire is that you have embraced this biblical principle in both mind and heart. This principle echoes consistently throughout the Bible, and let's explore a few key scriptures that emphasise it.

Matthew 10:39

39 Whoever finds his life will lose it, and whoever loses his life for my sake will find it.

John 3:30

30 He must increase, but I must decrease.

The Biblical principle here stands in stark contrast to the world's perspective. While the world believes in 'more is more' and scoffs at the idea of 'less is more,' for Christians, the concept of 'less is more with God' holds profound significance.

Today, we find John in a situation that challenges his certainty. He's imprisoned because he confronted Herod the tetrarch about marrying his brother's wife. This ordeal triggers doubt in John's mind—how could he, the forerunner of Christ, end up in jail?

His confidence in Jesus as the Messiah wavers, prompting him to send his disciples to question Jesus's identity.
Initially, John was certain of Jesus's identity when Jesus came to be baptised in the wilderness. He exclaimed, 'Look, the Lamb of God who takes away the sins of the world.' John was steadfast in his belief that Jesus was the Messiah, even when his own disciples started to question Jesus's role. Yet now in prison, John grapples with doubts about Jesus's role as the Messiah. John starts second guessing.

I'm sure there have been moments in your life when you've second guessed or questioned God's plans. So, this chapter will likely resonate with everyone. Let's start by reading our Scripture Matthew 11:2-11

2 When John heard in prison what Christ was doing, he sent his disciples

3 to ask him, "Are you the one who was to come, or should we expect someone else?"

4 Jesus replied, "Go back and report to John what you hear and see:

5 The blind receive sight, the lame walk, those who have leprosy are cured, the deaf hear, the dead are raised, and the good news is preached to the poor.

6 Blessed is the man who does not fall away on account of me."

7 As John's disciples were leaving, Jesus began to speak to the crowd about John: "What did you go out into the desert to see? A reed swayed by the wind?

8 If not, what did you go out to see? A man dressed in fine clothes? No, those who wear fine clothes are in kings' palaces.

9 Then what did you go out to see? A prophet? Yes, I tell you, and more than a prophet.

10 This is the one about whom it is written: "'I will send my messenger ahead of you, who will prepare your way before you.'

11 I tell you the truth: Among those born of women there has not risen anyone greater than John the Baptist; yet he who is least in the kingdom of heaven is greater than he.

We often expect God's will for our lives to follow a straightforward path, as we perceive "straight." Yet, God's path might involve some unexpected twists and turns. John ministered in the desert, preparing people for the coming Messiah and even had the privilege of baptising Jesus. After Jesus departed, John continued baptising in the region of Salim, as we saw in the previous chapter.

When John's disciples doubted Jesus, he stood firm in defending the faith, affirming that Jesus must increase while he must decrease. John's envisioned straight path likely involved ministering to the people in the countryside until the end of his days. Unexpectedly, his unwavering dedication to serving Christ led to imprisonment and, ultimately, execution by beheading.

This situation leads us to a poignant Scripture worth remembering, from Ecclesiastes 7:13

"Consider what God has done: Who can straighten what he has made crooked?"

Consider this: Sometimes, the journey toward becoming more like Christ involves a road filled with unexpected twists. Jesus, in the passage we just explored, lauds John the Baptist as unsurpassed among men. But how did he reach that acclaim? This wilderness preacher found himself imprisoned as a result of following Jesus, traversing an unforeseen, crooked path that left John questioning its purpose.

But here's the crux: God's concept of a straight path might not align with our own. What we perceive as chaotic, God sees as precisely right. In our human minds, we label it as a mess, while God simply asks, "Who knows better, Me or you?"

Consider the life of Christ—His intended path led through crooked terrain. It led Him on a detour to Golgotha's hill, where He would hang on a cross. How twisted a route for the King of Kings to face death on a cross. Yet, in the Father's eyes, this was the perfectly aligned path. So, why should our paths align with our definition of straight?

Jesus' response to John affirms that crooked paths are part of life's plan, reassuring him that He is indeed the Messiah. You need to pay attention to this, John sends his followers to Jesus, questioning His identity as the Messiah. And it's hard to believe that amidst their conversation, the disciples fail to mention John's imprisonment to Jesus.

Jesus, rather than promising a miraculous release, instructs them: "Go and report to John what you hear and see." Jesus highlights miraculous signs from the Old Testament: "The blind see, the lame walk, lepers are cleansed, the deaf hear, the dead are raised, and the poor receive good news." This serves as confirmation to John, aligning with scriptural prophecies and affirming Jesus as the Messiah. Everything unfolds according to the divine plan.

Isaiah 29:18

In that day the deaf will hear the words of the scroll, and out of gloom and darkness the eyes of the blind will see.

Isaiah 35:6

Then will the lame leap like a deer, and the mute tongue shout for joy...

Jesus confirms His identity as the Messiah through the evidence of miracles, yet He doesn't intervene to free John from prison. This might seem puzzling, considering Jesus could perform miracles, but it's crucial to understand that this path serves a higher purpose.
It draws John closer to God, fostering a deeper fellowship, despite John's confusion.

Jesus acknowledges John's greatness, emphasising the spiritual significance of John's current circumstances. This situation, although challenging, aligns with God's plan for John's spiritual growth and closeness to Him.

Jesus himself acknowledges at the end of this passage that among all who have been born, no one is greater than John the Baptist.

Romans 8:17

Now if we are children, then we are heirs-- heirs of God and co-heirs with Christ, if indeed we share in his sufferings in order that we may also share in his glory.

Perhaps in your life, God has kept you on a crooked path longer than you expected because He's moulding you into the likeness of His Son. Just as He worked in John's life, He might be doing the same in yours.

Verse 6 in our passage carries a crucial warning that demands our attention. Neglecting the understanding that following Jesus might lead to a difficult journey could cause stumbling in your Christian walk.

"Blessed is the person who does not stumble because of me." Matthew 11:6

In essence, those who struggle to grasp God's work in their lives are at risk. They may stumble and relegate their Christian faith to a secondary role.

Imagine this scenario: God places you on a crooked road, and you're baffled by His intentions in your life. As doubts creep in, you start convincing yourself that Christianity is too demanding, not worthwhile. Slowly, you distance yourself from God, thinking, "I signed up for Christianity; it should be smooth sailing from here." But then, you're thrown off by the unexpected crooked path.

However, those who comprehend that God occasionally leads them on winding roads experience substantial growth. This truth is evident when you read your Bible; God's ways often involve crooked paths.

Matthew 16:24

24 Then Jesus said to his disciples, "If anyone would come after me, he must deny himself and take up his cross and follow me.

Matthew 16:25

25 For whoever wants to save his life will lose it, but whoever loses his life for me will find it.

Today, some of you might find yourselves on a crooked road. This doesn't signify that God has forsaken you; rather, it indicates His desire to bless you by shaping you into the likeness of His Son. The crooked path isn't easy, but God provides the strength to navigate it. Always remember, with God, less is often more.

Abundant Blessings in Embracing "Less Is More"

"Therefore I tell you, do not worry about your life, what you will eat or drink; or about your body, what you will wear. Is not life more than food, and the body more than clothes? Look at the birds of the air; they do not sow or reap or store away in barns, and yet your heavenly Father feeds them. Are you not much more valuable than they? Can any one of you by worrying add a single hour to your life? And why do you worry about clothes? See how the flowers of the field grow. They do not labor or spin. Yet I tell you that not even Solomon in all his splendour was dressed like one of these. If that is how God clothes the grass of the field, which is here today and tomorrow is thrown into the fire, will he not much more clothe you —you of little faith? So do not worry, saying, 'What shall we eat?' or 'What shall we drink?' or 'What shall we wear?' For the pagans run after all these things, and your heavenly Father knows that you need them. But seek first his kingdom and his righteousness, and all these things will be given to you as well."

Matthew 6:25-33

Devotional:

Imagine a garden filled with various flowers, each displaying a unique beauty. Some gardens boast countless blooms of different hues, while others thrive with a select few. Yet, regardless of their number, each flower receives the nourishment it needs from the same sun and soil.

In life, we often equate abundance with having more—more possessions, more accomplishments, more on our to-do lists. But Jesus teaches us a powerful lesson in Matthew 6:25-33, revealing that in God's economy, less can indeed be more.

He uses the example of the birds of the air and the flowers of the field, highlighting how God cares for them without any worry or toil on their part. Just as these creations flourish without striving, God desires us to find contentment in Him, freeing us from the weight of unnecessary worries and pursuits.

In the same way that a garden flourishes when tended to with care and attention, our lives bloom when we seek God's kingdom above all else. When we prioritise our relationship with Him, aligning our hearts with His will, we find that our needs are met abundantly. God's provision surpasses our expectations, providing not just what we need, but beyond measure.

The key is seeking His kingdom first!

A principle that invites us to place our trust in God's perfect timing and provision.
It's an invitation to focus on what truly matters, rather than chasing after fleeting desires or anxieties.

Reflection:

Reflect on areas in your life where you may be striving for more, whether it's possessions, success, or approval. Consider how these pursuits may be hindering your ability to seek God's kingdom first. Are there worries or distractions that are weighing you down?

Prayer:

Heavenly Father, help me recognise the areas in my life where I'm seeking more instead of seeking You first. Grant me the wisdom to lay aside unnecessary worries and distractions, trusting in Your provision. Teach me to find contentment and joy in Your presence alone. In Jesus' name, Amen.

As you navigate your journey, remember that in God's hands, less can indeed lead to more— more peace, more contentment, and more of His abundant blessings.

Seven Days of prayer

Sunday: Unsaved Loved Ones
On this page, write down and Pray for the unsaved loved ones in your life. Ask God to open their hearts to His love and grace. Seek opportunities to share the Gospel with them through both words and actions.

Monday: Contentment

Here write down and Reflect on areas in your life where you seek more than you truly need. Pray for contentment and gratitude in the midst of abundance or scarcity, finding joy in what God has provided.

Tuesday: Surrender

Write down and Ask God to help you surrender any areas of your life where you are holding onto control. Pray for the wisdom to yield to His plans and trust in His perfect timing.

Wednesday: Distractions

Write down all your distractions then, Pray for the ability to identify and eliminate distractions that hinder your relationship with God. Ask for discernment to prioritise the things that truly matter in your spiritual journey.

Thursday: Humility

Write down and Reflect on areas where pride might be taking precedence. Pray for a humble heart that seeks to exalt God rather than self. Ask for strength to embrace humility in all aspects of life.

Friday: Spiritual Growth

Here write down the areas where you want grow, then Pray for spiritual growth and a deeper connection with God. Ask for wisdom to recognise His voice and guidance in your life. Seek a hunger for His Word and a thirst for His presence.

Day 7: Impact

Here write down all the areas in which you could serve, then Pray for God to use your life as a vessel for His purposes. Ask for opportunities to impact others positively, demonstrating the principle of "less is more" through your actions, words, and love.

Closing Thoughts

In concluding this journey through the pages of "Why Less Is Always More with Jesus," may we embrace the profound truth that simplicity and depth are not mutually exclusive in our walk with Him.

The lessons we've uncovered together reveal a counterintuitive reality: that in surrendering our desires for more, we gain immeasurable riches in our relationship with Jesus.

As we journey onward, let us continually seek the wisdom to discern between the world's clamour for excess and the divine invitation to embrace the abundance found in less. May we remember that the Kingdom of God often operates in the unassuming, the quiet, and the simple.

In the footsteps of John the Baptist, let us decrease so that He may increase in our lives. May our hearts be attuned to seek the beauty of simplicity, finding richness in the profound truths of God's love, grace, and mercy.

May this book serve as a reminder that less is indeed more—more peace, more depth, more intimacy with Jesus. As we close these pages, let us carry this truth forward, allowing it to shape our perspectives, decisions, and daily walk with the One who offers us abundant life in the most unexpected ways.

Remember, in the economy of God's Kingdom,

less is always more.

Blessings on your continued journey with Jesus,

Dave.

Notes

Notes

Notes

Notes

Notes

Notes

Notes

Notes

Other titles!

Dear Pastor

Dear Pastor is a heartfelt and inspiring devotional specifically crafted to provide encouragement, support, and spiritual nourishment to pastors who dedicate their lives to shepherding their congregations. In this carefully curated collection of daily reflections, each uniquely tailored to address the unique challenges and joys of pastoral ministry, author Pastor David Hancox offers a guiding hand and a compassionate voice to pastors on their sacred journey.

BE STILL : 31 Days Of Inspiration

Be Still: 31 Days of Inspiration" is a Christian devotional that invites readers on a transformative journey of faith, encouraging them to find solace, strength, and renewal in the presence of God. This collection of daily reflections provides a respite from the busyness of life, guiding readers to embrace stillness and seek intimacy with their Creator.

Available to purchase on Amazon.

Printed in Great Britain
by Amazon